FARRAR
STRAUS
GIROUX

ALSO BY LES MURRAY

The Vernacular Republic: Selected Poems

The Daylight Moon and Other Poems

The Rabbiter's Bounty: Collected Poems

The Boys Who Stole the Funeral: A Novel Sequence

Dog Fox Field

Translations from the Natural World

Subhuman Redneck Poems

Fredy Neptune: A Novel in Verse

Learning Human: Selected Poems

Conscious and Verbal

Poems the Size of Photographs

The Biplane Houses

The Biplane Houses

LES MURRAY

FARRAR, STRAUS AND GIROUX

NEW YORK

FARRAR, STRAUS AND GIROUX
19 Union Square West, New York 10003

Poems in this collection have previously appeared in *The Adelaide Review*, *The Age*, *Agenda*, *Antipodes*, *Ars Interpres*, *Australian Small Farmer*, *The Bridge*, *The Canberra Times*, *Carquinez Review*, *Commonweal*, *Daedalus*, *The Evansville Review*, *Harvard Review*, *The Herald* (Glasgow), *Literary Imagination*, *The Manhattan Review*, *Meanjin*, *The London Magazine*, *London Review of Books*, *The New Yorker*, *Poetry*, *PN Review*, *Poetry Scotland*, *Quadrant*, *Quarterly Essay*, *The Reader*, *The Rialto*, *Southerly*, *Subtropical*, *The Threepenny Review*, *The Times Literary Supplement*, and *The West Australian*. "The Newcastle Rounds" was commissioned by the Song Company for the Newcastle Festival, and several poems had their first airing in *The Full Dress*, National Gallery of Australia Publications, 2002.

Library of Congress Cataloging-in-Publication Data
Murray, Les A., 1938–
    The biplane houses / Les Murray. — 1st American ed.
      p. cm.
    ISBN-13: 978-0-374-11548-7 (hardcover : alk. paper)
    ISBN-10: 0-374-11548-6 (hardcover : alk. paper)
    I. Title.

PR9619.3.M83B54 2007
821'.914—dc22

                       2006031763

Designed by Cassandra J. Pappas

www.fsgbooks.com

1   3   5   7   9   10   8   6   4   2

To the glory of God

Contents

The Averted	*3*
Early Summer Hail with Rhymes in O	*4*
Post Mortem	*5*
The Hanging Gardens	*7*
Leaf Brims	*8*
Airscapes	*9*
The Statistics of Good	*11*
Twelve Poems	*12*
Too Often Round the Galleries	*14*
Travelling the British Roads	*15*
The Test	*18*
The Kitchen Grammars	*19*
Winter Winds	*20*
The Tune on Your Mind	*21*

The Domain of the Octopus	22
A Dialect History of Australia	26
For an Eightieth Birthday	27
On the Central Coast Line	28
Melbourne Pavement Coffee	29
Photographing Aspiration	31
Black Belt in Marital Arts	32
The Welter	33
A Levitation of Land	35
Through the Lattice Door	37
On the North Coast Line	38
The Nostril Songs	40
For a Convert in Boston	47
The Newcastle Rounds	48
The House Left in English	49
Yregami	50
Upright Clear Across	51
Ghost Story	53
The Shining Slopes and Planes	54
The Succession	55
A Stampede of the Sacrifice	56
The Offshore Island	58

An Acrophobe's Dragon   59

As Night-Dwelling Winter Approaches   60

The Hoaxist   61

Barker Unchained   62

The Cool Green   63

Lifestyle   65

Death from Exposure   66

Me and Je Reviens   67

Pressure   68

Church   69

Pastoral Sketches   70

Japanese Sword Blades in the British Museum   72

The Mare Out on the Road   73

The Blueprint   75

Blueprint II   76

Norfolk Island   77

Ends of the Earth   79

Birthplace   80

The Sick-Bags   81

Lateral Dimensions   82

Bright Lights on Earth   84

Panic Attack   85

Recognising the Derision as Fear   87

Gentrifical Force   88

The Physical Diaspora of William Wallace   89

The Brick Funnel   91

Sunday on a Country River   92

Ripe in the Arbours of the Nose   94

The Weatherproof Jungle Tree   96

Jet Propulsion Stereo   98

Industrial Relations   99

The Biplane Houses

The Averted

The one whose eyes
do not meet yours
is alone at heart
and looks where the dead look
for an ally in his cause.

Early Summer Hail with Rhymes in O

Suddenly the bush was America:
dark woods, and in them like snow.
The highway was miles of bath house,
bulk steam off ice shovelled over blue.
It was parallel shoals of Mikimoto,
glazy, banked, inching with pocked cars,
blindsided with vans slewed on water.
Had I not stopped off to buy plants
just back, mine could have been similar.
With unpredictable suns evaporating
I drove by guess in ancestral country
threading the white dark of afternoon.
Hills west of hills, twigs, hail to Dubbo,
all dunes of pursed constraint exhaling Ohh.

Post Mortem

I was upstaged in Nottingham
after reading poetry there
by what lay in the porter's room above:
ginger human skeletons. Eight of them.

Disturbed by extensions to the arts centre
and reassembled from the dozer's shove
some might have been my ancestors, Nottingham
being where my mother's people fled from

in the English Civil War.
These were older than that migration,
crusty little roundheads of sleep,
stick-bundles half burned to clay by water.

Their personhoods had gone, into the body
of that promise preached to them. What had stayed
in their bones were their diseases, the marks
of labour in a rope-furrowed shoulder blade,

their ages when they died, and what they'd eaten:
bread, bacon, beer, cheese, apples, greens,
no tomato atoms in them, no potatoeines,
no coffee yet, or tea, or aspirin

but alcoholic curds horn-spooned at a fair
and opium physic, and pease porridge.
The thought that in some cells their
programmes might persist, my far parentage,

attracted me no more than re-building
faces for them with wire and moulding.
Unsatisfied to go as a detective
to the past, I want the past live

with the body we have in the promise,
that book which opens when the story ends.
Being even a sound modern physique
is like owning an apartment in Venice.

The Hanging Gardens

High on the Gloucester road
just before it wriggles its hips
level with eagles down the gorge
into the coastal hills

there were five beige pea-chickens
sloping under the farm fence
in a nervous unison of head-tufts
up to the garden where they lived

then along the gutter and bank
adult birds, grazing in full serpent.
Their colours are too saturate and cool
to see at first with dryland eyes

trained to drab and ginger. No one here
believes in green deeply enough. In greens
so blue, so malachite. Animal cobalt too
and arrow bustles, those are unparalleled.

The wail lingers, and their cane
surrection of iridium plaques. Great spirits,
Hindoostan in the palette of New Zealand!
They don't succeed at feral.

Things rush them from dry grass.
Haggard teeth climb to them. World birds,
human birds, flown by their own volition
they led us to palaces.

Leaf Brims

A clerk looks again at a photo,
decides, puts it into a file box
which he then ties shut with string
and the truth is years away.

A Naval longboat is worked upstream
where jellied mirrors fracture light
all over sandstone river walls
and the truth is years away.

A one-inch baby clings to glass
on the rain side of a window as
a man halts, being led from office
but the truth is years away.

Our youngest were still child-size when
starched brims of the red lotus last
nodded over this pond in a sunny breeze
and the truth was years away.

Airscapes

The sky in flood. Marshalled on
by pressure, over the many-angled
windows of property far below.

The air has states, not places.
On the outer of Earth, the
sky above darkens to blue matter.

Lower than where Space streaks in,
risen scents and particles plateau,
diffusing to go worldwide.

The chill slates of that year
which, blown out of Iceland volcanoes,
famined up the French Revolution
hung and globed out on these levels.

Cloud wisps are an instructor
chalking to proof! And here it's true:
everyone has to have to.

These plunge lands being water dusts
that take colour from the Sun: gold cobble,
diaphanous frolic, optical liqueur.

A Thailand of cloud-dance,
cobalt gold-cracked cyclone Rumba
that raged half a province down its river
is now ten minutes' swell under wings.

The bubble-column of a desert whirlwind
fails, and plastic-bag ghosts
stay ascended, pallid and rare.

Over simmering wheat land,
over tree oils, scrub growing in rust
and way out to the storeyed Forties.

Here be carbons, screamed up
by the djinn of blue kohl highways
that have the whish of the world
for this scorch of A.D.

Tropopause, stratopause, Van Allen—
high floors of the world tower
which spores and points of charge
too minute to age climb off the planet.

A headlong space rock
discovers fiery retro jets
and adds to the earth above Earth.

The Statistics of Good

Chaplain General (R.C.)
Archbishop Mannix of Melbourne,
he who had a bog-oak footstool
so his slipper might touch Irish soil
first, when alighting from his carriage

saved, while a titular Major General
in the Australian Army, perhaps half
the fit men of a generation
from the shrapnelled sewer landscapes
of Flanders by twice winning close
referenda against their conscription.

How many men? Half a million? Who knows?
Goodness counts *each* and *theirs*.
Politics and Death chase the numbers.

Twelve Poems

That wasn't horses: that was
rain yawning to life in the night
on metal roofs.

—

Lying back so smugly
phallic, the ampersand
in the deckchair of itself.

—

Fish head-down in a bucket
wave their helpless fan feet.

—

Spirituality?
she snorted. And poetry?
They're like yellow and gold.

—

Being rushed through the streets
at dusk, by trees and rain, the
equinoctial gales!

—

The best love poems are known
as such to the lovers alone.

—

Creek pools, grown top heavy,
are speaking silver-age verse
through their gravel beards.

—

Have a heart: salted land
is caused by human tears.

—

Tired from understanding
life, the animals approach man
to be mystified.

—

A spider walking
in circles is celebrating
the birthday of logic.

—

To win me, they told me
all my bad attitudes
but they got them wrong.

—

Filling in a form
the simple man asks his mother
Mum, what sex are we?

Too Often Round the Galleries

Blokes and sheilas, copping lip,
walk the national comic strip.
Whitefellow art is half cartoons
and satire a picket line of goons.
Ridicule trumps justice, possums!

Travelling the British Roads

Climb out of mediaeval one-way
and roundabouts make knotted rope
of the minor British roads
but legal top speed on the rocketing
nickel motorway is a lower limit!
I do it, and lorries howl past me.

Sometimes after brown food
at a pub, I get so slow
that Highland trackways
only have one side
since they are for feet
and hoofs of pack horses
and passing is ceremony.

Nor is it plovers
which cry in the peopled glens
but General Wade's chainmen
shouting numbers for his road
not in the Gaelic scores
but in decimal English.

Universal roads return as shoal
late in the age of iron rims.
Stones in the top layer to be
no bigger than would fit in your mouth,
smiles John McAdam. *If in doubt*
test them with your lips!

Highwaymen, used to reining in
thoroughbreds along a quag of track,
suddenly hang, along new carriageways
or clink iron on needy slave-ships,
but wagon horses start surviving
seven years instead of three
at haulage between new smoke towns.

Then railways silence the white road.
A horseman rides alone between villages;
the odd gig, or phaeton;
smoke and music of the *bosh*
rising out of chestnut shade:
Gypsies, having a heyday.
Post roads, drying out, seem strange
beaches, that intersect each other.

When housemaids uncovered their hair
at windows, and a newfangled
steam roller made seersucker sounds
there were swans on the healed canal,
and with the sun came the Queen's
Horse Artillery in tight skeleton coats
to exercise their dubbined teams
watched by both fashionable sexes
in bloomer-like pedal pants.

I knew to be wary of the best dressed,
decent with the footsore,
but frontier-raffish with all
because the scripts they improvised from
were dry and arch, but quickly earnest.

From that day, and the audible
woodwind cry of peafowl, it was half
a long lifetime till jerked motors
would ripple the highroad
with their soundwaves, like a palate,
and kiss its gravel out
with round rubber lips
growling for the buckets of tar

and another life to the autobahn
nothing joins, where I race the mirror
in a fighter cockpit made posh
under flak of Guy Fawkes eve
over the cities of fumed brick.

The Test

How good is their best?
and how good is their rest?
The first is a question to be asked of an artist.
Both are the questions to be asked of a culture.

The Kitchen Grammars

The verb in a Sanscrit or Farsi
or Latin or Japanese sentence
most frequently comes last,
as if the ingredients and spices
only after collection, measure and
even preservation might get cooked.
To all these cuisines renown attaches.

It's the opening of a Celtic sentence
is a verb. And it was more fire and pot
for us very often than ingredients.
Had we not fed our severed heads on poetry
final might have been our fame's starvation.
Upholding cuisine for us are the French
to be counting in scores and called Gallic.

In English and many more, in Chinese
the verb surrounds itself nucleus-fashion
with its subjects and qualifiers.
Down every slope of the wok they go
to the spitting middle, to be sauced,
ladled, lidded, steamed, flipped back up,
becoming verbs themselves often

and the calm egg centres the meatloaf.

Winter Winds

Like appliqué on nothingness
like adjectives in hype
fallen bracts of the bougain-
magenta-and-faded-villea
eddy round the lee verandah
like flowers still partying
when their dress has gone home.

The Tune on Your Mind

Asperges me hyssopo
the snatch of plainsong went,
Thou sprinklest me with hyssop
was the clerical intent,
not *Asparagus with hiccups*
and never *autistic savant.*

Asperger, mais. Asperg is me.
The coin took years to drop:

Lectures instead of chat. The want
of people skills. The need for Rules.
Never towing a line from the Ship of Fools.
The avoided eyes. Great memory.
Horror not seeming to perturb—
Hyssop can be a bitter herb.

The Domain of the Octopus

The octopus east of here
lives in brackish water.
It doesn't hunt, but is fed.
Sand islands bulk in its craw.

A blue gut ferries tidewater
around them to bring it salt.
It digests escaped mill timber
and flat fish vacuum its floor.

Its branching arms go out
into real estate and farms,
around the leggings of forest
and to old lands undersea.

Dolphins, like 3D surfboards
born in the ocean, curvet
around fenced oyster gardens.
Power boats sit up to skim

between their wheels of water
and the oysters lid themselves
in their gnarled cups, against pressure.
A Boeing is going in the air

miles up, but will tinge the country
of the Octopus, and the Axe country.
The Octopus can build dams
of tide to suspend the Axe creeks

high when they are bankers
drifting with branches and rain
right to the foot of dead cowyards.
Then the Moon is pulled, and they drain.

Clouds go, and the sun comes together.
Over prawns' cellophane chatter
float leaves of the wild tobacco
and capsules grown in hill soil.

Lone boats lend their weight
to the agony of fish
who straighten water-coloured lines.
Elvers swim like moonlight inland.

In the Wallingat arm, only ever
deep enough for swans and bark canoes,
in the Octopus's south-hung belly
and all the shallowing bays

sunken sand-ripples are outlined
in pencilling of dark soil.
Miles of sill land are matt
bare inches above high water,

grassed tides that no longer fall.
Casuarina trees capture them,
wadded honey-blonde paperbark trees
and young palms like trashed venetians.

Octopus, rider of sea-level
up and down the Ice Ages:
once she embraced river ports
in still-unfocussed country

where black and white were extremes.
That merger of skins began a nation
soon snubbed out of existing.
One day its boat will come in.

This landscape of the Octopus
is itself a new settler
washed here and wave-rammed here,
younger than stories or man.

Slipway iron, and bushels
consigned to a horse-drawn Sydney
dissolve in her sand, but graves
and spearheads lie below it.

Octopus, infiller of coastline,
lengthener of rivers,
her image scientific and worldwide
but with that indigenous sound.

Old people with freed feet
and girls with new breasts wade
out into the Octopus,
and royally planing pelicans

ski to the Z of floating birds.
The Octopus can't love
but can be loved. Moon Man
swells, to raise sprinkling tribes

all along her arms
and over her belly. His tides
and prop-wash saw the earth
from under riverbank trees

and lay them down flooded and wrong.
The sun likewise, following,
takes sightings up every channel,
outreaching them for inland hill-cheeks.

A Dialect History of Australia

Bralgu. Kata Tjuta. Lutana.

Cape Leeuwin Abrolhos Groote Eylandt.

Botany Bay Cook Banksia Kangaroo Ground
Sydney Cove Broad Arrow Neutral Bay China Walls
Sodwalls Hungerford Cedar Party Tailem Bend
Jackadgery Loveday Darwin Kilmany. Come-by-Chance
Lower Plenty Eureka Darling Downs Dinner Plain
Telegraph Point Alice Maryfarms Diamantina
Combo Waterhole Delegate Federal Spion Kop
Hermannsburg Floreat Emu Heights. Pozieres
Monash Diggers Rest. Longreach The Gabba Hollow Tree
Perisher Police Point. Hawker Kuttabul Owens Gap
Greenslopes Repat. Red Bluff Curl Curl Charmhaven
Cracow York Kalimna Howrah. Wave Hill.
Beenleigh Yea Boort Iron Baron Long Pocket
Grange Nowhere Else Patho Tullamarine. Timor.

For an Eightieth Birthday

i.m. Lewis Deer

On a summer morning after the war
you're walking with the Belle of the Ball
both in your new pressed sports gear
over grass towards the scotching sound
of tennis balls on lined antbed
inside the netting's tall swarm.

You glance past the wartime rifle range
below the great cattle hill
that lifts your family name high
and into the gap the Japanese
soldiers never reached, there where
your years of farming will happen.

Bounce comes in your step from strung
racquets, from neighbours still young,
from unnoticed good of sun and birds
and the understandings calmly dancing
between you two, walking into the stroke-play
of gee-ups on a tournament Saturday.

On the Central Coast Line

When the magazine of rising suburbs
slips off my face, our train
has come down through shrubland

a head ahead

into a stone archipelago
of forested gigantic oysters
underlit to their mouth valves
in a river-coloured sea

a head a head
brushed to red cedar

We sail on steel at water level
and on and on up mirror fjord,
shell barges, roadless weekenders
in pastels turning khaki

don't let glances become
cells of a stare

We knock inside a tunnel
and are released to wide chrome,
to jelly-sting of wharf towns—

if that head turned
to show one certain face
this would not be now

Melbourne Pavement Coffee

Storeys over storeys without narrative
an estuarine vertical imperative
plugged into vast salt-pans of pavement
and higher hire over the river
ignited words pouring down live:

there an errant dog is running
nose down like a pursuit car
police car! police car! central city
and trams that look always oncoming
stop, and stand simmering like cymbals
after the mesh! of their pair.

Here posture is better, suitings thicker
and footmen are said to survive
behind oaks up the odd gravel drive.
We saw a wall of tomato
blazer-backs striped blue-and-yellow
ranged right across their school stage
just like an inland rain painting.

We heard our grandest parliament sigh
down Bourke Street *My country, why
did you leave me, and change at Albury?*
History made here touched the world.
Now a demoted capital bleeds politics
Burnet's immune system was right wing!
down the microphone, black icecream cone,
down the cinecamera, New Age monocle.

Not housing, but characterful houses
lace-trimmed like picnic day blouses
reigned when beer went with cray,
Now the crayfish are Formula One
cars, flat out in raging procession—
but we're off to where the river
learns and teaches the Bay.

Photographing Aspiration

Fume-glossed, unhearably shrill,
this car is dilated with a glaze
that will vanish before standstill—

and here's the youth swimming in space
above his whiplash motorcycle:
quadriplegia shows him its propped face—

after, he begged video scenes
not display his soaking jeans,
urine that leathers would have hidden

and the drag cars have engines on their engines.

Black Belt in Marital Arts

Pork hock and jellyfish. Poor cock.
King Henry had a marital block.
A dog in the manager? Don't mock!
Denial flows past Cairo.

A rhyme is a pun that knows where
to stop. Puns pique us with the glare
of worlds too coherent to bear
by any groan person.

Nothing moved him like her before.
It was like hymn and herbivore,
Serbs some are too acerbic for—
punning moves toward music.

The Welter

How deep is the weatherfront of time
that advances, roaring and calm
unendingly between *was* and *will be*?
A millisecond? A few hours? All secular life
worldwide, all consequences of past life
travel in it. It's weird to move ahead of,

so I went back to 1938,
the year of the Sesquicentennial,
and it was bare as a drought landscape
under a weakened sun. I found few objects,
a desiccated brougham in a slab lean-to,
a phrenological head defined in segments,

all sparse dead matter from far earlier times.
Underfoot at first were ghostly streets, but I
found my valley by its shapes. No trace of home.
My birth and my family were still travelling
in the time-front and beyond it. Mr. Speed,
the last convict, who had died that year

may be travelling too, in effects of his life.
All the human figures I thought I saw
away on that country proved to be
tall old-style window tombstones. I became
aware that all the clouds there'd ever been
were up ahead, being recycled in the life-front.

Beyond flat furrows and exhausted wire
salt frosted the cobble of parched waterholes.

But tears underlie every country. Nowhere do they
discharge the past, which is the live dark matter
that flows undismissably with us, and impends
unseen over every point we reach. One day

over wing-collared futures towered the dinosaur.

A Levitation of Land

OCTOBER 2002

Haze went from smoke-blue to beige
gradually, after midday.
The Inland was passing over
high up, and between the trees.
The north hills and the south hills
lost focus and faded away.

As the Inland was passing over
lungless flies quizzing road kill
got clogged with aerial plaster.
Familiar roads ended in vertical
paddocks unfenced in abstraction.
The sun was back to animating clay.

The whole ploughed fertile crescent
inside the ranges' long bow
offered up billion-tonne cargo
compound of hoofprints and debt,
stark street vistas, diesel and sweat.
This finest skim of drought particles

formed a lens, fuzzy with grind,
a shield the length of Northern Europe
and had the lift of a wing
which traffic of thermals kept amassing
over the mountains. Grist the shade
of kitchen blinds sprinkled every scene.

A dustbowl inverted in the sky
shared the coast out in bush-airfield sizes.
A surfer from the hundred-acre sea
landed on the beach's narrow squeak
and re-made his home town out of pastry.
A sense of brown snake in the air

and dogs whiffed, scanning their nosepaper.
Teenagers in the tan foreshortening
regained, for moments, their child voices,
and in double image, Vanuatu to New Zealand
an echo-Australia gathered out on the ocean
having once more scattered itself from its urn.

Through the Lattice Door

This house, in lattice to the eaves,
diagonals tacked across diagonals,

is cool as a bottle in wicker.
The sun, through stiff lozenge leaves,

prints verandahs in yellow Argyle.
Under human weight, the aged floorboards

are subtly joined, and walk with you;
French windows along them flicker.

In this former hospital's painted wards
lamplit crises have powdered to grief.

Inner walling, worn back to lead-blue,
stays moveless as the one person still

living here stands up from reading,
the one who returned here from her life,

up steps, inside the guesswork walls,
since in there love for her had persisted.

On the North Coast Line

The train coming on up the Coast
fitting like a snake into water
is fleeing the sacrificial crust
of suburbs built into fire forest.
Today, smoke towers above there.

We've winged along sills of the sea
we've traversed the Welsh and Geordie
placenames where pickaxe coughing
won coal from miners' crystal lungs.
No one aboard looks wealthy:

wives, non-drivers, Aborigines,
sun-crackled workers. The style
of country trains isn't lifestyle.
River levees round old chain gang towns
fall away behind our run of windows.

By cuttings like hangars filled with rock
to Stroud Road, and Stratford on the Avon,
both named by Robert Dawson, who ordered
convicts hung for drowning Native children
but the Governor stopped him. God

help especially the underdogs of underdogs
and the country now is spread hide
harnessed with sparse human things
and miles ahead, dawning into mind
under its approaching cobalt-inked

Chinese scroll of drape-fold mountains
waits Dawson's homesick Gloucester
where Catholics weren't allowed to live.
There people crowd out onto the platform
to blow smoke like a regiment, before windows

carry them on, as ivory phantoms
who might not quip, or sue,
between the haunches of the hills
where the landtaker Isabella Mary Kelly
(She poisons flour! Sleeps with bushrangers!

She flogs her convicts herself!)
refusing any man's protection
rode with pocket pistols. Which
on this coast, made her the Kelly
whom slander forced to bear the whole guilt,

when it was real, of European settlement.
Now her name gets misremembered:
Kelly's crossing, Kate Kelly's Crossing
and few battlers on this train
think they live in a European settlement

and on a platform down the first
subtropic river, patched velvet girls
get met by their mothers' lovers,
lawn bowlers step down clutching their nuclei
and a walking frame is hoisted yea! like swords.

The Nostril Songs

P. Ovidius Naso
when banished from Rome
remained in the city
for days on slave clothing,
for weeks in his study,
for decades in living noses—

—

Trees register the dog

and the dog receives the forest
as it trots toward the trees

then the sleeping tiger
reaches the dog en masse
before the dog reaches the tiger:

this from the Bengal forests
in the upper Kerosene age,

curry finger-lines in shock fur.

—

The woman in the scarlet tapestry
who stands up on a sprigged cushion
of land in space, is in fact
nude, as all are in the nostril-world.

What seem to be her rich gowns
are quotations from plants and animals
modulating her tucked, demure
but central olfactory heart

and her absent lover, pivoting
on his smaller salt heart
floats banner-like above her.

—

No stench is infra dog.

—

Fragrance stays measured,
stench bloats out of proportion:
even a rat-sized death,
not in contact with soil, is soon
a house-evacuating metal gas
in our sinuses; it boggles our gorge—
no saving that sofa:
give it a Viking funeral!

—

The kingdom of ghosts
has two nostril doors
like the McDonald's symbol.

You are summoned to breathe
the air of another time
that is home, that is desperate,
the tinctures, the sachets.

You yourself are a ghost.
If you were there
you are still there—

even if you're alive
out in the world of joking.

For the other species, the nasal kingdom
is as enslaved and barbed
as the urine stars around all territory,

as the coke lines of autumn
snorting into a truffle-pig's head

or the nose-gaffed stallion,
still an earner, who screams rising
for the tenth time in a day.

—

Mammal self-portraits
are everywhere, rubbed on
or sprayed on in an instant.

Read by nose, they don't give
the outline shapes demanded
by that wingless bird the human;

with our beak and eyes
we perceive them as smears
or turds, or nothing at all.

Painted from inside
these portraits give the inner
truth of their subject

with no reserve or lie.
Warned or comforted or stirred
every mammal's an unfoolable

connoisseur, with its fluids
primed to judge, as it moves
trapped in an endless exhibition.

—

Half the reason for streets,
they're to walk in the buzz
the sexes find vim in,
pheromones for the septa
of men and of women.

—

If my daddy isn't gone
and I smell his strength and care
I won't grow my secret hair
till a few years later on
on Tasmania. Down there.

—

When I was pregnant,
says your sister, my nose
suddenly went acute:
I smelled which jars and cartons
were opened, rooms away,
which neighbours were in oestrus,
the approach of death in sweat.
I smelled termites in house-framing
all through a town, that mealy taint.
It all became as terrible

as completely true gossip
would be. Then it faded,
as if my baby had learned
enough, and stopped its
strange unhuman education.

—

A teaspoon upside down
in your mouth, and chopping onions
will bring no tears to your cheeks.
The spoon need not be silver.

—

Draw the cork from the stoic age
and the nose is beer and whisky.
I'll drink wine and call myself sensitive!
was a jeer. And it could be risky.

Wesleyans boiled wine for Communion;
a necked paper bag was a tramp;
one glass of sweet sherry at Christmas,
one flagon for the fringe-dwellers' camp.

You rise to wine or you sink to it
was always its Anglo bouquet.

—

When we marched against the government
it would use its dispersant gas
Skunk Hour. Wretched, lingering experience.
When we marched on the neo-feudal
top firms, they sprayed an addictive

fine powder of a thousand hip names
that was bliss in your nostrils, in your head.
Just getting more erased our other causes
and it was kept illegal, to be dear,
and you could destroy yourself to buy it
or beg with your hands through the mesh,
self-selecting, as their chemists did say.

—

Mars having come nearest our planet
the spacecraft Beagle Two went
to probe and sniff and scan it
for life's irrefutable scent,
the gas older than bowels: methane,
strong marker of digestion from the start,
life-soup-thane, amoeba-thane, tree-thane.
Sensors would screen Ares' bouquet
for palaeo- or present micro-fartlets,
even one-in-a-trillion pico-partlets,
so advanced is the state of the art.
As Mars lit his match in high darkness
Beagle Two was jetting his way.

—

In the lanes of Hautgout
where foetor is rank
Gog smites and Pong strikes
black septums of iron
to keep the low down.
Ride through, nuzzle your pomander:
Don't bathe, I am come to Town:

Far ahead, soaps are rising,
bubble baths and midday soaps.
Death to Phew, taps for Hoh!
Cribs from your Cologne water.

—

Ylang ylang
elan élan
the nostril caves
that breathe stars in
and charm to Spring
the air du temps
tune wombs to sync
turn brut men on
Sir Right, so wrong—
scent, women's sense
its hunters gone
not its influence!
nose does not close
adieu sagesse

For a Convert in Boston

You've just resigned from judging

when trips to the night side of Venus
out of terror of her day,
and forgiveness of these, and concealment
while still saying Venus has a night side

have summoned the steel eagle-feathers
of antique armour to lisp
hotly through waxed rooms
of a pretend perfection.

But can you tell accused from victims?
As the broken faces come out,
aghast, through the pelting gauntlet,
they are added to the poor

and the night side of the poor.

The Newcastle Rounds

Tall sails went slack, so high did Nobbys stand
so they felled him in the surf to choke on sand
and convicts naked as legs in trousers
tunnelled for coal way below the houses.

Workers got wages and the Co-op Store,
wearing bowler hats as they waltzed through the door.
They danced in pumps and they struck with banners
and they ran us up a city with spans and spanners.

When Esssington Lewiss blew through his name
steel ran in rivers, coke marched in flame.
Wharfies handled wire rope bloody with jags
and took their hands home in Gladstone bags.

Then the town break-danced on earthquake feet
and tottered on crutches down every street.
We all sniffed coke back then, for pay,
but the city came up stately when the smoke blew away.

With horses up the valley and wines flowing down
clinking their glasses as a health to the town
freighters queued off the port at all times,
from pub to art show became a social sway,
the original people got a corner of a say
and the ocean spoke to surfers in whitecap rhymes.

The House Left in English

The house has stopped its desperate travelling.
It won't fly to New Orleans, or to Hungary again,
though it counts, and swears, in Magyar.

It is left in English with its life suspended,
meals in the freezer, clothes on airy shelves,
ski badges prickling a wall chart of the Alps.

The house plays radio, its lights clock on and off
but it won't answer the phone, even in Swiss German.
Since the second recession of helped steps

the house quotes from its life and can't explain:
dress-cutter's chalk. Melbourne Cup day 1950.
Alphorn skullcaps. Wartime soy flour, with an onion!

All earlier houses and times, in black and white,
are boxed by aged children visiting to dust this one
on its leafy corner and still, for a while, in colour.

Yregami

A warm stocking caught among limbs
evokes a country road
and tufted poodles growing out
on the paddocks sway like seared trunks.

Sliced whitefish bony with wind
and very high up recall an autumn day;
arrows showering far below them at a town
speed as flights of wires.

Glazed bush ballads rhymed in concrete
pose as modern office buildings
and a sated crowd leaving a ground
after a draw feels like a stage in love.

This horse seated on a chamber pot
swinging its head and forelock,
you'd swear it was a drunk old man.

Upright Clear Across

for Kay Alden

It's like when, every year, flooding
in our river would be first to cut
the two-lane Pacific Highway.
We kids would pedal down barefoot

to the long ripple of the causeway
and wade, deep in freezing fawn energy,
ahead of windscreens slashing rain.
We were all innocent authority.

The through traffic was mostly wise
enough not to try our back roads
so we'd draw the North Coast back together,
its trips, its mercy dashes, its loads,

slow-dancing up to our navel
maybe with a whole train of followers.
Each step was a stance, with the force
coming all from one side between shores.

Every landing brought us ten bobs and silver
and a facing lot with a bag on their motor
wanting us to prove again what we
had just proved, that the causeway was there.

We could have, but never did, lose our footing
or tangle in a drowning fence

from which wire might be cut for towing—
and then bridges came, high level,
and ant-logs sailed on beneath affluence.

Ghost Story

Two cars, converging by chance
follow the same near-empty roads
into the city after midnight.
Suburban miles and the streetlamps
moon pearls, or at hot salute,
the traffic lights all on green.

Just before mobile phones
this is. They turn the same corners
all through the insider streets:
twice the far-back lights shorten
interval, but aren't let overtake.
An hour, now, since the mountains.

The lead car does a sudden
sideslip, and swerves to the kerb,
at bay in a sleep avenue
of steeping houses. The other
slows past it, and itself turns
in at that exact driveway.

Open. Shut. Its driver climbs
the front yard terraces, not looking.
He keys the front door and goes in.
Light for a while deep inside.
The silhouetted sit, dimmed,

for a quarter of an hour,
then a shovelling of coral
from furtive downhill treads
till their motor starts starting.

The Shining Slopes and Planes

Having tacked loose tin panels
of the car shed together,
Peter the carpenter walks straight up
the ladder, no hands,
and buttons down lapels of the roof.

Now his light weight is on the house
overhead, and then he's back down
bearing long straps of a wiry green
Alpine grass, root-woven, fine as fur
that has grown in our metal rain gutters.

Bird-seeded, or fetched by the wind
it has had twenty years up there
being nourished on cloud-dust, on washings
of radiant iron, on nesting debris
in which pinch-sized trees had also sprouted.

Now it tangles on the ground. And the laundry
drips jowls of coloured weight
below one walking stucco stucco
up and down overlaps, to fix
the biplane houses of Australia.

The Succession

A llama stood in Hannover, with a man
collecting euros for its sustenance.
The camelid had a warm gaze. Its profound
wool was spun of the dry cloud of heaven.

My fingers ached with cold in October.
I had to fly on to Great Britain.
There the climate spared them, and Guy Fawkes
dotted on for weeks, pop, Somme and flare,

as if the wars of tabloid against Crown
were swelling up to a bitter day in Whitehall—
but battle never burst out from under the horizon.
Leaves and cock pheasants went dizzily to their fall:

the birds often stuck like eyebrows to the road.
They and grouse, shot, were four bob at the butchers
long ago when we'd wintered at Culloden.
Two and a scavenged swede, and we were fed.

Back then we weren't quite foreign, and the Dole
called on us at home. Our own country's hard welfare
made this a prodigy to us, like reverse arrest!
When the media are king, will only fear be civil?

A Stampede of the Sacrifice

ST. VALENTINE'S DAY 1916

Starting to realise, blaming sergeant majordom
five thousand Light Horse recruits break camp
unarmed, but in their strapping uniform.

A raw division of infantry, augmenting hubbub,
joins their tramp into Liverpool, the Army suburb.
It is ten months since the Gallipoli landing
but chevrons or shoulders exhorting or commanding
can't restrain this khaki spasm.

Yelling rather than intelligible, mobs fall
on hotels and drink them, pump, keg and bottle.
From rattling glass, men fill their blue canteens
and, shouting endearments, surge to commandeer
steam trains to the city. Frightened women
crowd off, and hobble-run to hide in churches.

Reports of the day don't allow individuals speech
as they rampage. But while all manhood can't say
converges in a braying roar, it maintains purchase.
The strikers smash every foreign word on display:
Belgium, Diesel, lingerie, Rassmussen—
glass under hobnails, signs poxed of their enamel.
All this has been deleted from the legend.

MP whistles and an unrepeated fusillade
are noises off. Hansom cabs bolt. But the riot
starts collapsing from strain of too much meaning.
Men not finding their murderer start sightseeing.

A few who know they joined up lightly change
clothes in unguarded shops. But they're likely few.
Most simply exhaust their range,
put things down, and start returning.

Slippage, plum jam, licked pencils of review.
The newspapers of then are quickly warned to silence.
Sentences re-emerge, not least through courts martial:
a thousand get sent home, or sent to gaol,
before the Trenches reconnect their ravenous cable.

Many of those dismissed will invent new names
and rejoin the shipped battalions urging forward
where private disaster is bestially swapped by men.
For fifty years, pubs close at six against them.

The Offshore Island

Terra cotta of old rock undergirds
this mile of haze-green island
whitening odd edges of the sea.

It is unbrowsed by hoofed beasts
and their dung has not been on it.
Trees of the ice age have stayed rare

though no more firesticks come out
from the long smoky continent
lying a canoe-struggle to the west.

The knee-high bush is silvered canes,
bracken, unburnt grasses, bitou.
Miners came, and ate the mutton birds.

Greeks camped out there in lean times
fishing. Their Greek islands lived in town
with their families. Now it's National Park.

The world shrinks as it fills.
Outer niches revert to space, in which
to settle is soon too something.

An Acrophobe's Dragon

Shepherds on opium and rum
were jeered for their blue dragons
up the pioneer Tableland.

The oldest road off that plateau
steepens into blued dragon-knee
switchbacks, on the ocean pitch of fall

behind saplings in the sky,
bared cliffs out there like seraphim
and trees the wool teamsters chained

to brace their tipping see-saw
drays down the further thousands.
Height toils up to you like Bolivia

and nods without a side glance.
Decades teetering above brinks
of death and rebirth stay unsaid

like the brake-failing literal plunge
all shriek-prayers upside down.
Down, off the last tongue of asphalt

convict-laid gravel purrs way east
along rivers and a single file of farms
vivid between knitting slopes of bush.

As Night-Dwelling Winter Approaches

Tree shadows, longer now, lie
across the roads all one way
but water goes fluently switchback,
swelling left, unbuttoning right
over successive cement fords.

Cattle walk their egrets around
but other long-beaked pensive birds
of the low damp places
snatch off the ground, rise above
stress of the plovers, and start flying

north over the world to sing.

The Hoaxist

Whatever sanctifies itself draws me.
Whether I come by bus or Net,
rage and fun are strapped around my body.

I don't kill civilians. I terrorize
experts and the elites. I drink their bubbly,
I wander among their principles

then at a pull of my cord
I implode. And laughter cascades in,
flooding those who suddenly abhor me.

The media, who are Columbine
with their prom queens and jocks,
unsheathe their public functions

and prolong the drowning frenzy.
(Strange that the owners should want to
sell the Herald to the Baptist church.)

Sometimes my cord has to be pulled
for me by others. Or I cut it off.
A buried hoax can be a career, a literature—

Ah Koepenick! Oh Malley! My Ossianic Celts
brought us the Romantic Era,
my Piltdowns can resurge as stars!

Barker Unchained

for Ian Keast, teacher of English

Around the hilly roads
I thought of you delivering
Western culture day by day
into impassive mailboxes,
tinny tip-front ones, milk cans,
shot beer-fridges, hard stoic slots,
sweet pairs entwined at the leg.
Nothing of it was junk mail
at the moment of receipt,
though much would have short life;
there'd be odd bright returns,
though, and thank-you pumpkins.

I see you on very back roads
where tyres snore on gravel
and your propellant dust
catching up at every stop
enrolls you in a khaki furore.
But sling it all now. Park the van,
return the mailbags to prison
and post yourselves off to where
you're a man of your own letters.

The Cool Green

Money just a means to our ends?
No. We are terms in its logic.
Money is an alien.

Millions eat garbage without it.
Money too can be starved
but we also die for it then,
so who is the servant?

Its weakest forms wear retro disguise:
subtly hued engraved portraits
of kings, achievers, women in the Liberty cap,
warlords who put new nations on the map—

but money is never seen nude.
Credit cards, bullion, bare numbers,
electronic, in columnar files
are only expressions of it,
and we are money's genitals.

The more invisible the money
the vaster and swifter its action,
exchanging us for shopping malls,
rewriting us as cities and style.

If I were king, how often
would I come up tails?
Only half the time
really? With all my severed heads?

Our waking dreams feature money everywhere
but in our sleeping dreams
it is strange and rare.

How did money capture life
away from poetry, ideology, religion?
It didn't want our souls.

Lifestyle

In the stacked cities
they dance the Narrow Kitchen
barista, barista!
we go to wear black.

barista, barista!
will you cook in your kitchen?
will you drink in your suit?
will you come on the Net?

Once it was unions
now it's no carbohydrates,
no fats, then no proteins
barista, barista!

In the tall cities
barista, barista!
world is not made of atoms
world is made of careers.

Death from Exposure

That winter. We missed her stark face
at work. Days till she was found, under

his verandah. Even student torturers
used to go in awe. She had zero small talk.

It made no sense she had his key.
It made no sense all she could have

done. Depression exhausts the mind.
She phones, no response, she drives up

straight to his place in the mountains,
down a side road, frost all day.

You knock. What next? You can't manage
what next. Back at last, he finds her car.

She's crawled in, under, among the firewood.
Quite often the world is not round.

Me and Je Reviens

My great grand-uncle invented haute couture. Tiens,
I am related to Je Reviens!

It is the line of Worth, Grandmother's family
that excuses me from chic. It's been done for me.

When Worths from Coolongolook, Aboriginal and white,
came out of Fromelles trenches on leave from the fight

they went up to Paris and daringly located
the House of Worth. At the doors, they hesitated—

but were swept from inquiry to welcome to magnificence:
You have come around the world to rescue France,

dear cousins. Nothing is too good for you!
Feast now and every visit. Make us your rendezvous.

I checked this with Worths, the senior ones still living:
Didn't you know that? they said. *Don't you know anything?*

Pressure

A man with a neutral face
in the great migration
clutching his shined suitcase
queueing at the Customs station:

Please (yes, you) open your suitcase.
He may not have understood.
Make it snappy. Open it! Come on!
Looking down out of focus did no good.

Tell him to open his suitcase!
The languages behind him were pressure.
He hugged his case in stark reluctance.
Tell him put suitcase on the counter!

Hasps popped, cut cords fell clear
and there was nothing in the suitcase.

Church

i.m. Joseph Brodsky

The wish to be right
has decamped in large numbers
but some come to God
in hopes of being wrong.

High on the end wall hangs
the Gospel, from before he was books.
All judging ends in his fix,
all, including his own.

He rose out of Jewish,
not English evolution
and he said the lamp he held
aloft to all nations was Jewish.

Freedom still eats freedom,
justice eats justice, love—
even love. One retarded man said
church makes me want to be naughty,

but naked in a muddy trench
with many thousands, someone's saying
the true god gives his flesh and blood.
Idols demand yours off you.

Pastoral Sketches

The sex of a stallion at rest
bulges in subtle fine rehearsal,
and his progeny drop in the grass
like little loose bagpipes.
Wet nap and knotty drones, they lie
glazing, and learning air,
then they lever upright, wobbling.
Narrow as two dimensions
they nuzzle their mothers' groin
for the yoghurt that makes girth.

—

The prickly paperbark tree
annually called Snow-in-summer
resembles the fragrant coiffure
of a crowd of senior women;
it joins up into a mountain,
white as Graz, warm as cauliflower.
Pencil holes in the clay soil
are where cicadas woke from their
years of foetus life, to two
two days frantic amethystine.

—

Individuals move round, miles apart,
planning gravel, making access.
Local news is the kind least sold.
Funerals come by radio or phone,
deduction and For Sale bring other bits,
some must even be danced for
at the Hall. *You know Sid's moved?—
Where to?—Out Gunnedah.—*

After only eighty years?—His absence
will be the dark under their house brim.

                    –

Cleome flowers on improbably lank
spears incline their heads, to fling
free of the booty weight of bees.
Cats freeze and dab, and have to be
screamed back No, Mogg! as a snake
shuffles its suits like a cardsharp's stretch.
Christmas stars detonating violetly
the season comes on with beachwear and bling.
We preferred the no-fly zone of Spring,
and cattle wade in their peaceful tragedy.

Japanese Sword Blades in the British Museum

Merciless whitewater craft
keel-upwards in long curve,
hammered to a dancing edge:

each with its furniture removed
they surmount black cloth
in a parade of glass cases
all down this shadowy hall—

and yet they are in battle
with little winking cameras,
blood star, steel flash.

Why, I said to Yojimbo, this
is an exhibition of lightnings!

The Mare Out on the Road

Sliding round the corner on gravel
and there was a mare across the road
and a steep embankment down to the paddock.
The moment was crammed with just two choices.

Sliding fast, with the brakes shoaling gravel.
Five metres down, and would the car capsize?
The moment was crammed with just two choices.
One of two accidents would have to happen.

The poor horse was a beautiful innocent
but her owner never let a grudge go by.
No court case, just family slurs for life.
Sliding fast with the brakes shoaling gravel.

The mare was expanding. Would she run?
leave a gap before or behind to drive through?
No chance. She grew in moist astonishment.
Five metres down, and would the car capsize?

Blood hoof collision would be NOW, without a swerve.
Would the car explode in flames, below? It plunged
aslant, away down. The door groaned up like a hatch.
No court case, just family slurs for life

because the old man didn't believe in accidents,
nor in gestures. The mare trots off
ahead of boots hobbling to find the old man's son.
The poor horse was a beautiful innocent.

The breeder's son on their tractor
was full of apologies and shame, winching
the mouth-full, glass-weeping car back up in secret
because the old man didn't believe in accidents.

The Blueprint

Whatever the great religions offer
it is afterlife their people want:
Heaven, Paradise, higher reincarnations,
together or apart—
for these they will love God, or butter Karma.

Afterlife. Wherever it already exists
people will crawl into ships' framework
or suffocate in truck containers to reach it,
they will conjure it down
on their beaches and their pooled clay streets,
inject it, marry into it.

The secular withholds any obeisance
that is aimed upwards.
It must go declaratively down,
but "an accident of consciousness
between two eternities of oblivion"—
all of us have done one
of those eternities already, on our ear.

After the second, we require an afterlife
greater and stranger than science gives us now,
life like, then unlike
what mortal life has been.

Blueprint II

Life after death
with all the difficult people
away in a separate felicity.

Norfolk Island

What did they get for England,
the Bounty mutineers?
Tahitian wives, then the discharging
of murder, on an islet walled by sea.

When all the ship-takers were dead
England gave their descendants
this greater island draped like a green
parachute over cliffs and ravines

and pegged with towering furled pines.
All around lay the same blue wall
supplies are still roped and lightered
in over, for the Beauty mountaineers.

They lived in an abandoned gulag.
Trim Georgian houses whose inside
fireplaces astonished the first
of Bounty's neo-Polynesians.

On a Sydney whim, they were driven
out of that guilty settlement:
damn half breeds on Quality Row!
Sick people in their beds on the street—

Go up and live on your allotments!
Now the island is a garden city
in the flown-over ocean,
a godly tan aristocracy

whose children don't seem hostile
and cars buzz them around
their anxiously fostering nation
of big unused fields.

*(Chorus) We got
everything Tahiti got
e-e-xcept the
coconut!*

Ends of the Earth

Motor knitting a small wake
on sea detailed with ice
a fisherman smokes out
a long compound word

meaning backless drums
and sandflies caught
in bear-grease on a face.

—

Knees up under mossed
turf of an Iceland farm roof
were just gable ends
for twenty generations
before the disco opened there.

—

Gravel outwash rivers
less deep than stilt thigh-boots
but cold as anaesthetic

and an uncollective figure
with a bow wave, knife-throwing
gleamy loops at the flow.

Birthplace

Right in that house over there
an atom of sharp spilled my sanctum
and I was extruded, brain cuff,
in my terror, in my soap.

My heart wrung its two
already working hands together
but all the other animals
started waking up in my body,

the stale-water frog, the starving-worm;
my nerves' knotwork globe
was filling up with panic writing;
bat wings in my chest caught fire

and I screamed in comic hiccups
all before focus, in the blazing cold—
then I was re-plugged, amid soothe,
on to a new blood that tasted.

Nothing else intense
happened to us, in this village.
My two years' schooltime here
were my last in my own culture,

the one I still get held to
in this place, in working hours.
I love the wry equal humane
and drive in to be held to it.

The Sick-Bags

We landed through a Southerly Buster,
mad wind of thirty degrees south.
This landing was truly foot and mouth:
the sick-bags whispered out of every seat as
the plane bucked through two thousand metres,
lurched, and caused a grim fluster
like massed fans at a cotillon
before wheels locked, and rolled
and we would live on.
Heads of young trees were at work
still brushing the ground.

Lateral Dimensions

Cloudy night—
not enough stars
to make frost

haunted house—
one room the cattle
never would go in

mowing done—
each thing's a ship again
on a wide green harbour

purification—
newspapers soaked in rain
before they are read

an airliner, high—
life falling in from space
to ramify

rodeo bull
he wins every time
then back on the truck

only one car
of your amber necklace
holds a once-living passenger

afternoon plains—
the only hill ahead
is the rising moon

eels'
liquid jostle through the grass
that night of the year

big pelican, begging,
hook through one yellow foot—
and nobody dares

on line
the first motor car
trotting without a horse

joking
in a foreign language
everyone looks down

accused of history
many decide
not to know any

all the colours
of inside a pumpkin—
Mallee forest in rain

Bright Lights on Earth

Luminous electric grist
brushed over the night world:
White Korea, Dark Korea,
tofu detailing all Japan,
Bangkok on a diamond saddle,
snowed-in Java and Bali
circled by shadow isles,
Cairo in its crushed-ice coupe,
dazzling cobwebbed Europe
that we've seen go black.

Now the streetlights don't
switch off for wars. The past
is fuel of glacé continents,
it rims them in stung salt,
Australia in her sparsely starred
flag hammock. Human light
is the building whose walls
are inside. It bleeds the planet
but who could be refused
the glaring milk of earth?

Panic Attack

The body had a nightmare.
Awake. No need of the movie.

No need of light, to keep hips
and shoulders rotating in bed
on the gimbals of wet eyes.

Pounding heart, chest pains—
should it be the right arm hurting?

The brain was a void
or a blasted-out chamber—
shreds of speech in there,
shatters of lust and prayer.

No one can face their heart
or turn their back on it.

Bowel stumbled to bowl,
emptied, and emptied again
till the gut was a train
crawling in its own tunnel,

slowly dragging the nightmare
down with it, below heart level.
You would not have died

the fear had been too great
but: to miss the ambulance moment—

Relax. In time, your hourglass
will be reversed again.

Recognising the Derision as Fear

Death gets into the suburbs, but sleek
turnover highrise keeps it out of mind

and wilderness, wrapped in its own deaths,
scarcely points us at ours,

but furred rusty machines, and grey
boards unglazed for heritage or holiday—

you can't truck in enough bricks.
Settled country is the land of the dead,

there you are taught love as mourning,
you shop in boarded-up places.

It's great to follow car-dust
out towards the Mistake,

way past a working people's farm,
long widowed, standing in space.

Gentrifical Force

Gentrifical force, gentrifical force:
that's an ex-convict on his own horse
with a new white wife and the black one gone
with his first children to a far station.

Then race and real estate took a joint course
and white ladies held the no-mixing line
that ran up through sheaves to raise the bricks
which would become every rising town.

Gentrifical force turned Prunty to Brontë
and shipped myriads more to colonial bounty
where some, abashed to be safe on the fringe,
still feed wars and guilts to their cultural cringe.

Gentrifical force: who paid for yours?
I sold out the soldiers and made them go mad
when we were rewritten by a new fashion.
I had to be cool. I have no remorse.

From the high ground we still tell our blood
that they are scum, living on stolen salt land—
Gentrifical force leaves so many behind
and turns them to primitives in its mind.

The Physical Diaspora of William Wallace

Your conquest of the world
by merchandrie and steam,
by logic and surgery
gets my sidelong esteem

but every true nation is
underlain by hard men.
I fought for a kingdom
to guard our ways in.

We'd fought off each other,
we'd fought off the Norse;
I chain-maced the English
from my wee shaggy horse

and my heart's near the Highlands,
my spleen is in York,
one gnawed shin's in London,
my blood's in your talk—

such was their peace-work.
I confess I brought grue
down on cottars and lassies
but for less long than you

with your borderless realms
of doctrine and idea,
often colder than the cleavers
that sent me far and near,

me, followed by high-hearts,
the headlong and the poor
to Wembley and Calcutta,
to Melbourne and Bras d'Or

to be Scots for some lifetimes
and then Scots no more.

The Brick Funnel

Down-slope to the yellow brick school
ran a wealth of houses.
One was like a grounded moustache,
one like a baked apple made of felt, and smoking,
one like a great cloth over an uncleared feast.

There was a house blinding among trees
like a portholed arrival on earth, and one
sooty inside, with saké drums and big radishes.
There was a lockable ocean view, and tall
pigeonhole cliffs densely populated by TV,

and a training house populated only by explosions.
Lower down, a domestic fo'c's'le lay propped
leaking levels of sun, and stone apartments
shared their alley washdays. The door
of a tufa dugout was outlined in blue.

Looking uphill from the yellow brick school
there were only carport bungalows
ascending the same hillside.

Sunday on a Country River

After caramel airs of the sugar islands
and their carrying-handle bridges,
we skimmed over salt rainwater
that was reached across by smoke.

Ospreys flew, or sat up castled on sticks
and the shore trees were algal with creeper.
The diked low country on parole from floods
began foreshadowing inland jacaranda.

Below a two-deck bridge and cathedral city
water silver-brown as polarized shades
shook ahead of us, and split
in two behind us like innumerable catch.

We tied up under high oiled gondola poles.
Fig trees had star-burst the pavements we pubbed on
but the blackboards lunch was scrubbed on
sent us away to cast off for more vista.

Pelicans still luffed aloft
now into air that breathed of cattle, and
front-verandah houses, bland with equality,
perched atop increasing bluffs.

Only a historic Bedouin tent of vast
corrugated iron presided, farther back,
and turning under layered cliffs
we kept causing long wing-skitter takeoffs.

We were nearly to Pages', when our boat
bumped and started cavilling. *It gets hairy from here,*
we said. And there was hair, too,
muddy blonde, growing just underwater.

Ripe in the Arbours of the Nose

Even rippled with sun
the greens of a citrus grove darken
like ocean deepening from shore.
Each tree is full of shade.

A shadowy fast spiral through
and a crow's transfixed an orange
to carry off and mine
its latitudes and longitudes
till they're a parched void scrotum.

Al-Andalus has an orange grove
planted in rows and shaven above
to form an unwalkable dream lawn
viewed from loggias.
                              One level down,
radiance in a fruit-roofed ambulatory.

Mandarin, if I didn't eat you
how could you ever see the sun?
(Even I will never see it
except in blue translation).

Shedding its spiral pith helmet
an orange is an irrigation
of rupture and bouquet
rocking the lower head about;

one of the milder borders
of the just endurable
is the squint taste of a lemon,

and it was limes, of dark tooled green
which forgave the barefoot sailors
bringing citrus to new dry lands.

Cumquat, you bitter quip,
let a rat make jam of you
in her beardy house.

Blood oranges, children!
raspberry blood in the glass:
look for the five o'clock shadow
on their cheeks.
                        Those are full of blood,
and easy: only pick the ones that
relax off in your hand.

Below Hollywood, as everywhere
the trees of each grove appear
as fantastically open
treasure sacks, tied only at the ground.

The Weatherproof Jungle Tree

for Margaret Woodward's new hen-house

Pointed at bow and poop
or plumed with flourish astern
chickens crowd out of their coop
with a scratch and a half-turn
into the footwork of forage
unless hailed on by grain,

grain first scattered in the Stone Age
to secure their eggs and meat
by having their cluck around the village,
their filigree down round our feet
and their panic failure of inference
about those we grabbed. So neat.

But everything comes home to roost
now, and points at us with spears;
for our battery Belsens
a virus could be unloosed
at us out of the East
by the mild poultry, it appears—

but it may succumb to research,
and if not, horrors pass
and sometime again, fowls will perch
as here, in a weatherproof tree,
a rococo excretory palace
with all its hatching boxes

safe from snakes and from foxes
since, after this red-meat hiatus,
fowls will be back in their billions
because we redesigned their nests,
evolving their breeding, like ours,
up out of the sudden-death grass.

Jet Propulsion Stereo

Over Westminster Bridge
a cobalt B1 bomber
curved upward with doughboys,
GIs and Hemingways; it
circled up on spread wings
then racked them back
like a man pushing down
hard on a top rafter
to boost into speed,
dwindle westwards and be haze
at the end of the Cold War.

Above Waterloo Bridge
in a different year
Concorde was rising
atop ear-drilling stereo
over the ranked city's
mid stream. Far up, white,
near vertical, it looked
like the cropped writing-quill
Martin Waldseemüller would dip
to letter on his draft map
the wrong tribute-name *America*.

Industrial Relations

Said the conjuror Could I have afforded
to resign on the spot when you ordered
me to saw the Fat Lady
in half before payday
I would have. I find wage cuts sordid.